THE TRIANGLE FACTORY FIRE

BY VICTORIA SHERROW

Spotlight on American History
The Millbrook Press • Brookfield, Connecticut

TO MY FATHER, CHARLES, WITH LOVE

Cover photograph courtesy of The Bettmann Archive
Photographs courtesy of Brown Brothers: pp. 6, 30, 42, 45, 52;
UPI/Bettmann: pp. 9, 39, 49; The Bettmann Archive: pp. 12, 16,
18, 21, 23; Wide World Photos: p. 54; Ginger Giles: p. 54 (inset).

Library of Congress Cataloging-in-Publication Data
Sherrow, Victoria.
The Triangle factory fire / by Victoria Sherrow.
p.   cm.—(Spotlight on American history)
Includes bibliographical references and index.
Summary: Describes the 1911 fire at the Triangle Shirtwaist
factory in New York, the conditions surrounding the disaster,
and its effect on industrial safety after the event.
ISBN 1-56294-572-6 (lib. bdg.)
1. Triangle Shirtwaist Company—Fire, 1911—Juvenile literature.
2. Clothing factories—New York (N.Y.)—Safety measures—
History—20th century—Juvenile literature.   3. Industrial safety
—New York (N.Y.)—History—20th century—Juvenile literature.
4. New York (N.Y.)—History—1898–1951—Juvenile literature.
[1. Triangle Shirtwaist Company—Fire, 1911.   2. Industrial safety
—History.] I. Title. II. Series.
F128.5.S23 1995
363.37′9—dc20   95-14523   CIP   AC

Published by The Millbrook Press, Inc.
2 Old New Milford Road, Brookfield, Connecticut 06804

CONTENTS

Chapter One
Trapped!
7

Chapter Two
Six Dollars a Week
11

Chapter Three
Union, Hand in Hand
19

Chapter Four
"We Strike for Justice"
28

Chapter Five
Tragedy
35

Chapter Six
A Shriek of Despair
44

Chapter Seven
Crusade for Safety
49

Chronology
56

Further Reading
58

Bibliography
59

Index
62

THE TRIANGLE FACTORY FIRE

The Triangle Shirtwaist Factory was located on the top 3 floors of the Asch Building. When the fire broke out, many workers could not be rescued because the ladders reached only to the sixth floor.

TRAPPED! 1

Something was terribly wrong at the Joseph J. Asch building, located on the Lower East Side of New York City. Late in the afternoon of Saturday, March 25, 1911, people in the streets were startled by a sound like an explosion. Then came the noise of shattering glass. Black smoke began billowing from windows on the eighth floor. A man on the street ran to the corner and pulled Fire Alarm Box 289. Word spread throughout Washington Square— "Fire! There's a fire!" It was then 4:45 P.M.

The top three floors of the ten-story, dark gray Asch Building housed the Triangle Shirtwaist Company. It employed about five hundred workers. The Triangle factory made a type of woman's cotton shirt called a shirtwaist, with puffed sleeves, a collar, buttons down the front, and a fitted waist. Shirtwaists had been very popular since 1895. Thousands of workers were making them in factories like the Triangle.

People rushed toward the corner of Greene Street and Washington Place. Within a few minutes, it was clear that both the eighth and ninth floors of the building were ablaze.

Aghast, the crowds watched as girls stood in the windows, screaming or begging for help, their skirts on fire. From the ninth floor, a dark object that looked like a bundle of fabric came hurtling to the ground. People gasped when they realized that it was the body of a teenage girl. She had chosen to jump rather than be burned to death. Other workers came to the window ledges. Flames reached out toward their hair and clothing.

Within minutes, firemen arrived. The white horses pulling the fire wagons neighed and jerked at the reins, upset by the noise and the strong smell of blood. Desperate workers watched as the firemen raised their ladders. To everyone's dismay, the ladders only reached to the sixth floor, short of the stranded victims.

Meanwhile, other workers had rushed to the building's one fire escape. As they fled down the steps, the weak metal broke, and they went crashing hundreds of feet to the ground.

An onlooker, Louis Waldman, would later write, "Horrified and helpless, the crowds looked up at the burning building, saw girl after girl appear at the reddened windows, pause for a terrified moment, and then leap to the pavement below. . . ." A cashier who had escaped from the building said, "They hit the sidewalk spread out and still."

William Gunn Shepherd, a reporter from the United Press, was another eyewitness. As the tragedy unfolded, he telephoned the story to his office. He wrote, "Down come the bodies in a shower, burning, smoking, flaming bodies. . . . The floods of water from the firemen's hoses that ran into the gutter were actually red with blood."

When the flames were finally out, 146 people, mostly young women, lay dead. Most were poor immigrants from Russia, Italy, Hungary, Germany, Austria, and Ireland. They had known hard-

View of the ruins following the fire. Many workers jumped from the windows to their deaths rather than be consumed by the flames.

ship in America, living with their families in shabby tenements and working long hours, six and seven days a week, for low pay.

The Triangle fire shocked New Yorkers and moved the government to action. Hundreds of thousands of people joined a massive funeral march for the victims. Protest meetings were held, and citizens donated money for the victims' families. Over the next few years, new fire laws were passed in New York and in other states. The disaster also energized the labor movement, which had been growing steadily through the years. More workers joined unions so they could bargain for better working conditions.

Improvements came only after much suffering. In the years before the Triangle fire, thousands of other factory workers had died because of fires and dangerous equipment and conditions. In 1910, there had been forty-two fires in shirtwaist factories alone. While some people were surprised by the Triangle fire, others had seen it coming for years. They had warned the public and the government about the risks that workers faced every day. Now, with 146 people dead, their fears had become a reality.

The poor conditions and low wages at the Triangle Company were typical of American factories during the early 1900s. Businesses took advantage of the many poor people who needed work. The lowest-paid workers were often women and children.

Before the Industrial Revolution, most women who earned wages worked either at home or as servants in other people's houses. Some women earned money by doing extra spinning or weaving at home. Others did "piecework." Women, and sometimes their children, shelled nuts, made artificial flowers and hats, sewed trimmings on hats, and assembled coats and jackets.

During the late 1700s, such jobs began to move from homes to factories. By the 1800s, factories were making textiles (cloth), shoes, clothing, and other goods. Poor women and children became the main employees at textile factories.

When Samuel Slater opened his first textile mill in Rhode Island, in 1790, his workers included nine children aged seven to eleven. In the years that followed, millions of children worked in factories. They carried coal and made cigarettes and cloth. In canning factories they snipped beans, shelled peas, and husked corn. Many were crippled by dangerous machinery. Some died.

[11]

Child laborers were a common sight in the late nineteenth and early twentieth centuries, when laws did not exist to prevent taking advantage of children.

By 1820, half of the workers in one Rhode Island mill were children of nine and ten. They worked twelve to thirteen hours a day, six days a week, earning from thirty-three to sixty-seven cents a week. By the 1820s, many new mills were operating, chiefly with the help of "factory girls," as they were called. By the late 1830s, women working in mills in Lowell, Massachusetts, earned about $1.75 a week after paying the $1.45 fee for room and board. Workers started before seven each morning and stopped between five and seven at night, with two half-hour breaks for meals.

Critics of the growing factory system worried about how it would affect human lives. "The factory system contains in itself the elements of slavery," said an 1846 article in *The Voice of Industry*.

During the mid-1800s, millions of immigrants came to America. They fled from hunger, poverty, and political and religious persecution in Europe and Asia. By 1880, about half a million people were arriving each year.

Immigrants were a large, cheap source of labor. Immigrant men worked in coal mines, steel mills, meat-processing plants, and canneries, as well as in construction and on railroads.

AMERICAN CITIES grew rapidly, with many poor people living in run-down neighborhoods called slums. A typical slum apartment building (or tenement) stood six stories high. Each floor had about fourteen rooms, but only a few rooms had windows. The others were dark, airless, and foul-smelling. On hot summer nights, tenants often slept on the roofs or fire escapes.

Rooms were crowded. Many families took in relatives or boarders to help pay the rent. Six to eight people might live in one small room. One newspaper reporter found twelve people sleeping in a basement room less than 13 feet (4 meters) square.

Housing codes, seldom strict, were rarely enforced. Tenement owners broke laws regarding plumbing, electricity, and fire safety. The apartments had no toilets or bathtubs. Few had sinks or hot water. Sewers and outhouses were not maintained.

Even in a run-down tenement, rent cost more than most poor wage earners made in a month. Between 1870 and 1890, the number of women and children in the workplace rose by 88 percent. Some women were the sole support for themselves or their families. They worked in offices, laundries, cotton or woolen mills, or restaurants, but most women worked in wealthier people's homes as servants.

Second to them in number were women who lacked other job skills, but knew how to sew. They were known as "sewing women." About one fourth of the women working in factories were immigrants, and a few were Native Americans. African-American women were often refused factory jobs. If hired, they were obliged to do the most dirty, difficult work.

By 1910, about 7,400,000 women in America—more than 20 percent of all women—worked outside the home. Most city women worked in garment factories, often called sweatshops because workers had to "sweat"—work very hard. Most factories were located in old buildings, in airless, crowded spaces. Workers roasted in the summer and shivered in the winter. Employers often mistreated or harassed them. For a ten- to twelve-hour day, six or seven days a week, they earned from $4 to $9 a week.

A reporter for *Leslie's Illustrated Weekly* wrote:

Pass along any of our great commercial thoroughfares and you will see displayed in the show-windows suits of clothes for sale at $5, $6, $7, $8, $9, and $10. You marvel,

How can they do it? . . . A sweater's shop is a place where clothing is made for the big dealers at the prices that enable them to undersell their rivals and offer garments so wonderfully cheap, and it is in addition a graveyard for youth and hope.

Like tenement apartments, sweatshops were always uncomfortable and often unsafe. The Triangle Company operated from the top floors of its building. Factory owners preferred top floors because rents were cheaper, and they could also save money by using sunlight instead of relying on gas jets and electricity. The eighth floor at the Triangle held a cutting room, where workers cut pieces of cloth for the sleeves, fronts, and backs of blouses. On the ninth floor were 240 sewing machines set in 16 tightly packed rows. Workers sat at these rows of machines with their chairs back to back. The tenth floor held offices and crates for packing and shipping garments.

At the Triangle factory, children ran errands, sorted buttons, threaded needles, and cut threads, among other tasks. The youngest workers earned $1.50 for a seven-day week. Laws banned children under age fourteen from factory work, but many companies broke the law. Now and then, city inspectors came into the Triangle shop. Underaged workers were hidden in crates and covered with fabric or clothing until the inspectors left.

New shirtwaist employees of ages thirteen and fourteen might start as messengers but could become button sewers, earning $6.00 a week. By age sixteen, fast, skillful workers might be running machines for $9 a week, with a top rate of about $12.

Pauline Newman, who began working at the Triangle factory in 1901, later became a union leader. In 1975 she recalled:

Workers toiled long hours for little pay in cramped, dirty factories known as sweatshops.

The corner of the shop would resemble a kindergarten because we were young, eight, nine, ten years old. . . . It was a world of greed; the human being didn't mean anything. The hours were from 7:30 in the morning to 6:30 at night when it wasn't busy. When the season was on we worked until 9 o'clock. No overtime pay, not even supper money. There was a bakery in the garment center that produced little apple pies the size of this ashtray and that was what we got for our overtime instead of money.

Triangle supervisors watched workers closely to make sure they did not stop their tasks. Toilets were located outside the factory, and workers had only a few minutes to use them. A heavy steel door leading to the hall and stairwell was kept locked. Employers said work must not be "interrupted."

Garment workers had to pay for thread and electricity, for the chairs or boxes they sat on at work, and for the use of coat lockers. Clocks were often set back in time so that workers could not see how much overtime they had worked. Some workers were paid by the piece of work produced, rather than with a fixed, weekly salary. Often, if a worker became skilled and worked quite fast, the employer lowered her payment per piece. A pot-bellied stove in the middle of the factory provided scant heat in the winter. Drinking water came from a dirty tap in the hall.

Clara Lemlich described conditions at her factory in the November 28, 1909, issue of the *New York Evening Journal:*

> The shops are unsanitary—that's the word that's generally used, but there ought to be a worse one used. Whenever we tear or damage any of the goods we sew on, or whenever it is found damaged after we are through with it, whether we have done it or not, we are charged for the piece, and sometimes for a whole yard of the material. At the beginning of every slow season, $2 is deducted from our salaries. We have never been able to find out what this is for.

Under such conditions, factory workers produced finished garments. Shirtwaists, worn all over America, often with a long, dark skirt, were the height of fashion. The shirtwaist business had made many men rich. Factory owners lived in large, well-furnished homes staffed by servants. Their children wore fine clothes and enjoyed excellent food, schools, toys, vacations, and all sorts of luxuries.

Life was quite different for the workers. Pauline Newman says:

For American women, shirtwaists were a very popular item of clothing from about 1800 to 1919.

Most of the women rarely took more than $6.00 a week home, most less. . . . I lived in a two-room tenement with my mother and two sisters and the bedroom had no windows. . . . We wore cheap clothes, lived in cheap tenements, ate cheap food. There was nothing to look forward to, nothing to expect the next day to be better.

UNION, HAND IN HAND 3

Starting in the early days of America, workers tried to improve their lives. People in the same type of job formed groups called trade unions. Some unions held strikes, in which a large number of employees refused to work until certain demands were met. These activities grew into the American labor movement.

In the 1700s unions were local, with small-scale activities. They were not well organized. But workers began to see that they could increase their power by bargaining as a group. Collective bargaining gave workers more power than they had as individuals.

A Philadelphia shoemakers' union held the first well-organized strike in 1799. Printers in various cities also formed unions, followed by tailors, shipbuilders, and others. Throughout the 1800s, miners held unsuccessful strikes.

By the early 1800s, workers knew high profits were being made from their labor. They hoped for better wages and working conditions. During these years, most union members were men. Women were kept out of higher-paying jobs, so they were not welcome in unions for skilled workers. Many male workers did not think women should be in the labor force at all. They kept women out of unions.

[19]

There were other reasons women did not join unions. They were raised to be obedient and to avoid conflicts. Some saw themselves as temporary workers who would quit after marriage. Unskilled women knew they were easy to replace. They often lived on the brink of starvation, terrified of losing their jobs.

Even so, some women became pioneers in the labor movement. Women started their own unions, led strikes, and took part in walkouts in a number of states. In 1824, in Pawtucket, Rhode Island, about one hundred women weavers joined male workers to protest wage cuts and longer working hours. The next year, women formed the United Tailoresses Society of New York. They held a five-week strike in 1831, the first known all-woman strike in America. Their demands were refused, though, and the strike ended. Women workers were encouraged by a strike held in 1834. Millworkers in Lowell, Massachusetts, gained a twelve-hour workday. Branches of the Lowell Female Labor Reform Association were started in other New England mill towns.

Workers still sought to shorten the workday, at least to ten hours. They resented working seventy-three hours a week for less than a dollar. Some business owners simply changed factory clocks so workers would think they were leaving an hour earlier. Sometimes workers also had trouble collecting their pay. To deal with such concerns, the Ladies' Industry Association tried to unite sewing women in 1845, but this group was short-lived.

Women workers discussed their problems at a mass meeting in New York City in 1863. The next year, sewing women started the Working Women's Union (WWU). Their motto was: "Union, hand in hand."

The Working Women's Union organized money-raising events and group picnics. Dues were collected to help workers in trouble

Children and striking workers helped draw
attention to the need for new labor laws.

and to build up "strike funds," money to aid workers who were on
strike. WWU members sometimes attended meetings of the New
York Trades' Assembly, a large men's union that included workers
from many trades and different local unions.

Sewing women in Baltimore, Chicago, Detroit, and Buffalo,
New York, formed unions. A Philadelphia group published the
Women's Journal and gained a 20 percent pay raise for its members.
A Boston newspaper said, "Let such unions be formed among sew-
ing women everywhere. They are sure to succeed if they are in
real earnest as spunky women know how to be."

Workers tried to reform the contract system, which lowered their wages. A contractor was hired by factories or the government to deliver a certain number of garments. He then hired women workers to sew them, paying them very little. During the Civil War, union sewing women visited President Abraham Lincoln and explained their plight. They told him that contractors received $1.75 per dozen shirts but paid workers only $1.00. Lincoln told the government official in charge of clothing contracts to make sure that women workers received fair wages.

In 1865, the *New York Sun* newspaper invited working women to describe their problems at a public meeting. Hundreds of citizens listened to women who earned eleven to seventeen cents for twelve hours' work. The workers often slept only a few hours a night and got through the day with one cup of tea and a slice of bread. Some had to support children or invalid husbands.

After the meeting, workers and prominent citizens formed the Working Women's Protective Union (WWPU). Middle- and upper-class women aimed to empower working women with free legal aid. Between 1865 and 1890, this union handled more than 27,000 complaints and recovered $24,647 due to women workers who sought their help. The organization also supported a law that fined employers who did not pay their workers.

MEANWHILE, America's manufacturing industries were growing. In 1860, more than a billion dollars were invested in manufacturing. About 1.5 million Americans were working in factories. More people were competing for jobs, and some workers found their wages growing smaller each year, not larger. More newspapers were published for working people, some written in foreign languages. *The Labor Standard, The Workingman's Advocate, Welcome*

Young working women could not afford much more than a small room to live in and meager meals to eat.

Workingman, and *National Labor Tribune* encouraged workers and told them about progress in the labor movement.

The National Labor Union (NLU) was formed in 1866. The union noted the special needs of working women and called sewing women the "daughters of toil of the land." NLU leaders urged women to unionize and to demand equal pay for equal work.

Working women were joined by suffragists—people who thought women should have the right to vote, as men did. Suffragists said that by voting, women could improve the laws and elect people who would help workers.

At the 1869 convention of the National Labor Union, one of the delegates was Susan B. Anthony, a leading suffragist who had helped found the Working Women's Protective Union. But many men resented her playing such a visible role. In 1870, in spite of opposition, a woman from the Sewing Girls Union of Chicago was elected as second vice president of the National Labor Union. The NLU had begun to break up by this time. But it had raised women's awareness of labor issues and increased their interest in unions.

Upset by low wages, more women in the sewing trades were joining unions. They continued to work to get rid of middlemen who took a large share of their wages. Sewing women also developed self-help projects. In New York City, middle-class women formed the Shirt Sewers' Cooperative Union to improve wages.

A new association of labor unions, mostly male, was also growing. The Knights of Labor had been started in Philadelphia in 1869 by Uriah Stephens, a tailor educated as a Baptist minister. By 1886, the Knights had 750,000 members. It had persuaded one group of railroad owners to restore cut wages. During the 1880s, their leader, Terence Powderly, said that factory owners could control their workers "as though the slave ship had dumped its load of human chattel on the floor of the factory."

In 1886, the American Federation of Labor (AFL) was formed. The AFL was made up of various smaller unions of skilled workers. The group supported equal pay for women workers. Women were allowed to join, but again, few women held skilled jobs. The male-dominated system of apprenticeship kept women from training for skilled jobs. Low wages made it hard for women to pay dues. AFL meetings were often held in back rooms of saloons, and meetings might last far into the night. Women who had chores and children at home were not likely to attend.

In general, women were denied leadership positions. People of color were not welcome in the AFL either. Bigotry against women, African Americans, Asians, and others kept many workers from improving their skills and incomes.

During the late 1800s, the public heard numerous pleas on behalf of poor workers. In 1891, Pope Leo XIII criticized the "hard-heartedness of employers and the greed of unchecked competition" and said, "A small number of very rich men have been able to lay upon the teeming masses of the laboring poor a yoke little better than slavery itself."

THE NUMBER of women workers reached 5.5 million by 1900. America was now the world's leading industrial nation. New machines and inventions—the electric light, telephone, typewriter—and better transportation systems boosted America's ability to produce, ship, and sell goods. More than 12 million immigrants came between 1890 and 1910.

Workers welcomed a 1902 report by the U.S. Industrial Commission. It said that too many work hours each week led to lower production, poorer quality work, higher operating costs, and health hazards. The commission recommended a shorter workday. During this time, union members often sang these verses at meetings:

We want to feel the sunshine;
We want to smell the flowers;
We're sure that God has willed it,
And we mean to have eight hours.
We're summoning our forces
From shipyard, shop, and mill,
Eight hours for work;
Eight hours for rest;
Eight hours for what we will!

"These People Are Part of My Machinery"

ALTHOUGH SOME BUSINESS owners paid fair wages to their workers and cared about their safety, many did not. During the mid-1800s, one New England mill owner said,

So long as my hired hands do my work for what I choose to pay them, I keep them, getting out of them all I can. What they do or how they are outside my walls, I don't know nor do I consider it my business to know. They must look out for themselves as I do for myself. When my machines get old and useless, I reject them and get new ones and these people are part of my machinery.

As the labor movement grew, many employers warned workers not to join unions. Some required new workers to sign an "ironclad," a contract stating they would never join a labor union. Workers who did join, or who were suspected of being union members, were often fired. There was also blacklisting, in which employers circulated lists of people who were in unions to make sure that no one would hire them.

Throughout America, employers also used mistrust to divide workers and keep them from cooperating with each other. They encouraged workers of one nationality to dislike those from a different religious or ethnic background. In that way, they could drive people apart and so prevent them from uniting against employers.

Despite the commission's report and many appeals to employers and the public, workers' lives remained grim. By 1900, women garment workers were roused to build their own strong union and fight for better working conditions.

The owners at many factories banned unions and threatened to fire workers who joined. This and other barriers kept women away from unions. In 1895, only 5 percent of all union members in America were women. But as a new century dawned, more women supported unions. Some, including Triangle Company workers, joined in secret. Women soon made up more than half of the membership of shirtwaist and laundry unions.

In 1900, women from different garment trades united to form the International Ladies' Garment Workers' Union (ILGWU). The American Federation of Labor approved this union, which included makers of shirtwaists, children's clothing, caps, and other garments. The ILGWU pledged to protect their rights.

More help came in 1905. Middle- and upper-class reformers joined workers to start the Women's Trade Union League (WTUL) in New York City. The league pledged to improve wages and conditions "for those women who are not being treated fairly." Members included prominent society leaders, such as Eleanor Roosevelt and Mrs. O.H.P. Belmont. They joined workers like Mary Anderson, who later became director of the Women's Bureau of the U.S. Labor Department, and seamstress Rose Schneiderman, who also became a well-known labor leader.

By 1907, the WTLU had organized many workers from different jobs. It sponsored public speeches and provided money, food, and clothing to women who were having a hard time making ends meet. The trade union opened places called "rest rooms" downtown where waitresses could relax between shifts. Women doctors provided free health care to members. WTUL meetings were held near places where women lived and worked.

Still, not much changed for shirtwaist workers. They continued to toil long weeks for low pay in dangerous, unsanitary buildings. During 1908, many shirtwaist workers grew increasingly resentful and walked out from their jobs in protest.

*I*N 1909, there were five hundred shirtwaist factories in New York City alone. They employed more than 30,000 workers. Triangle workers had been meeting secretly with leaders of their branch of the ILGWU, Local No. 25 Waistmakers' Union, founded in 1906. When the Triangle's owners found out, the supervisors told workers that there was no longer enough work for them at the factory.

Soon, the fired workers saw that the factory had placed ads in the newspaper for more shirtwaist workers. Enraged, they flocked to the office of Local No. 25 to make plans. As Alice Henry wrote in *The Trade Union Woman:*

> The [fired workers] picketed the shop, and told the girls who answered the advertisement that the shop was on strike. The company retaliated by hiring thugs to intimi-

Once women began organizing to demand better working conditions and higher pay, they became a powerful force.

date the girls, and for several weeks the picketing girls were being constantly attacked and beaten. These melees were followed by wholesale arrests of strikers, from a dozen to twenty girls being arrested daily.

About five hundred workers joined the strike within twenty-four hours. As the workers left the Triangle factory the next day, they found police already waiting on the sidewalk. One officer, brandishing his nightstick, told a worker, "If you don't behave, you'll get this on your head."

Workers were advised to go to a nearby hall where members of the Women's Trade Union League discussed picketing laws and the most effective way to run a picket line. They were told to speak quietly, not to threaten anyone, and to avoid touching anybody who approached them. They were also urged to write down the number of any policeman who arrested them and give it to a union officer.

On November 22, hundreds of workers and union officials and supporters filled the auditorium of Cooper Union, a tuition-free college nearby. Famous labor leader Samuel Gompers, president of the American Federation of Labor, said that he had never declared a strike in his life. But he saw good reasons for this one.

One of the most eloquent speakers that evening was teenager Clara Lemlich. She had already joined several strikes and was recovering from a severe beating she had received during one of them. After listening to other, more cautious, speakers, Lemlich urged workers to go forward and declare a general strike, not a shop-by-shop strike. The whole shirtwaist industry must take part or manufacturers would not listen. Pledging to strike, Lemlich took an oath, saying, "If I turn traitor to the cause I now pledge, may this hand wither from the arm I now raise." Throughout the hall, workers echoed the oath.

The strike gained momentum as thousands of shirtwaist workers joined the union and the picket lines. Soon, newspapers were calling it "The Uprising of the 20,000." Among them was Pauline Newman, who later said, "Thousands upon thousands left the factories from every side, all of them walking down toward Union Square." Altogether, 30,000 workers may have taken part. Many were teenage girls. The strike joined women and men, Italians, Russians, Irish, Czechs, Hungarians, and native-born Americans— all for a common cause.

THOSE WERE difficult weeks. Workers marched in the cold, holding up signs that read:

GIVE US A 52-HOUR WORKWEEK.

WE NEED MORE FIRE ESCAPES.

WE STRIKE FOR JUSTICE.

Strikers were also insulted and beaten by thugs hired by the factory. Police arrested picketers, sometimes for no reason. By Christmas, 723 strikers had been arrested. Many were taken to Blackwell's Island prison for two weeks where they scrubbed floors and shared cells with violent offenders. Many were fined. The union raised funds to pay fines and get people out of jail.

More help came from the New York Women's Trade Union League. League leaders collected more than $40,000 in relief funds. League members volunteered to stand with Triangle workers on the picket lines. They protested unlawful arrests and endured the same abuse as the workers. Mary Dreier, a well-known society woman and WTUL leader, was arrested. When a police-man realized who she was, he apologized and asked, "Why didn't you tell me you was a rich lady?" Newspaper publicity about this incident helped the strikers.

Newspaper articles explained why workers were striking and described police abuse. On December 4, a long line of shirtwaist strikers went to City Hall to ask the mayor for police protection. As people outside of New York heard about the strike, it spread to Philadelphia and other cities.

The public lent some support. A group of several hundred actresses announced that they would buy and wear only union-made shirtwaists. Women at Vassar and Wellesley colleges sent money to help the strikers. Wellesley students promised to buy a thousand shirtwaists made by a cooperative garment company, one in which employees owned a share of the business.

Some smaller shirtwaist companies decided to settle the strike. They signed agreements to permit unions in their shops and to stop charging employees for supplies. They agreed to a fifty-two-hour workweek and limits on overtime. As a result, thousands of shirtwaist workers returned to their jobs.

The Triangle and other large factories held out. As the strike went on, money was badly needed. The union sent representatives to raise money by speaking to women's groups and unions in other cities. Alone, with a borrowed suitcase, Pauline Newman went to Buffalo, New York, then to Rochester and Syracuse. She returned with six hundred dollars for strikers and their families. Other women traveled to Washington, D.C., to New England, and to Pennsylvania.

Some prominent New Yorkers helped workers to organize a large fund-raising meeting. In her *Diary of a Shirtwaist Striker*, Theresa Malkiel wrote that most of the working women walked both ways to the meeting, skipping dinner, so they could donate money for the cause. Of the $300 collected, $70 was in pennies.

The large shirtwaist companies next tried to hire black women as strikebreakers. Black women had long been excluded from these jobs. The few who did work in shirtwaist factories had joined the strike. Mary White Ovington, one of the founders of the National Association for the Advancement of Colored People (NAACP), heard about the plans. She told members of the Cosmopolitan Club, a group of African-American and white community leaders. That group urged black women not to let themselves be used as strikebreakers. It also urged the ILGWU to help black women gain jobs after the strike ended and to include them as union members.

By January 22, 1910, the Leiserson Company and Bijou Waist Company had accepted workers' demands. Most of the shirtwaist companies joined them, agreeing to a fifty-two- or fifty-four-hour workweek and higher wages. They also agreed to paid holidays and a half-day workday on Saturday. The strike was declared over on February 15.

Much good came from the strike. It proved that women could stand firm and be outstanding leaders. The strike raised group spirit and increased membership in the garment workers' union by many thousands of people. It paved the way for later successes, such as a strike in which about 60,000 ILGWU members, mostly male cloakmakers, won a fifty-hour workweek and better pay.

But the Triangle's owners, Max Blanck and Isaac Harris, refused to bargain with the union. During the strike, they found enough nonunion workers willing to cross picket lines and work for them. When the strike ended, the Triangle workers were no better off than before. They still had the same wages and a fifty-nine-hour workweek. Their building remained unsanitary and unsafe.

TRAGEDY 5

During the shirtwaist strike, Triangle workers had demanded improved fire safety. They asked the owners to keep doors unlocked on the eighth, ninth, and tenth floors and to install working fire escapes. There had been four fires at the factory in just ten years. The Diamond Waist Company, run by the same owners, had had fires in 1906, 1909, and 1910.

Firefighters had long worried about the sweatshops on the Lower East Side. During a fire on Canal Street, an assistant fire chief had died. Fire Chief Edward Croker had been pushing for new laws and strict enforcement. An organized group of businessmen opposed him, objecting to the increased costs of sprinkler systems, new fire escapes, and other improvements.

Chief Croker asked them to at least have regular fire drills and teach employees about fire prevention. A fire prevention expert offered to give factory workers a fire safety education program. The Triangle factory owners and others refused the offer.

Speaking to a New York State Assembly investigating committee on December 28, 1910, Chief Croker explained that the fire department could only reach a fire seven stories high (about 85 feet, or 26 meters). When Judge M. Linn Bruce asked him, "Is this a serious danger?" Croker replied that thousands of people worked in buildings "with absolutely not one fire protection, without any means of escape in case of fire."

In November 1910, twenty-five workers in a Newark, New Jersey, factory died during a fire. Nineteen jumped from the windows of upper floors. Chief Croker warned that conditions were ripe for a similar tragedy in New York City, saying, "A fire in the daytime would be accompanied by a terrible loss of life."

Fire officials criticized the owners of the Asch Building and the Triangle factory, but nothing was done. On the eve of the fire, doors were still being kept locked. The stairway in the building was narrow—only 33 inches (84 centimeters) across. The hall that led to the door was lined with large rag bins. There were no sprinklers and only one old fire escape.

THE TRIANGLE FIRE began on the eighth floor about the time the bells rang to turn off the power, between 4:30 and 4:45 P.M. The fabric cutters on that floor, all men, had gone. Nearly 500 women were still at the factory. About 130 women on the eighth floor were preparing to collect their pay and leave. Some machine operators on the ninth floor were moving toward the washrooms. As always, they would then walk past a supervisor with their purses open to show that they had not stolen anything. Since it was Saturday, people looked forward to being with their families or friends or going shopping.

Instead, workers soon found themselves trapped in a blazing building. The fire may have started when a match or cigarette butt was tossed too close to a pile of cloth scraps. Or sparks may have come from a defective machine motor part.

Once started, the fire spread quickly. The work tables, set up for the next day, held piles of sheer fabric and tissue paper patterns. These were easy prey for the flames that now shot from table to table. Flames engulfed the lines of finished shirtwaists that hung in the room and raced under the tables where wicker baskets held scraps and lace. The fire ravaged bolts of cloth and bins of muslin scraps. The bins, which had not been emptied for a few weeks, held more than 2,000 pounds (907 kilograms) of scraps. The heat rose as the fire spread.

Seeing the flames, workers and male supervisors grabbed buckets and filled them with water from an open barrel. They dragged a fire hose into the room from the hallway. But when they opened the valve, there was no water pressure. Their efforts hopeless, they soon quit and planned ways to escape.

Before leaving, switchboard operator Dinah Lifschitz called the ninth floor to warn the 270 workers there about the fire. Nobody answered. She reached workers on the tenth floor. The company's bookkeeper called the fire department.

By now, many workers knew they faced an emergency. Escape was hindered by the rows of tightly packed chairs and machines. No fire drill had ever been held at the factory.

A survivor, Rosie Safran, later said,

I heard somebody cry *'Fire!'* I left everything and ran for the door on the Washington Place side. The door was locked and immediately there was a great jam of girls before it. The fire was on the other side, driving us away from the only door that the bosses had left open for us to use in going in or out. They had the doors locked all the time. The fire had started on our floor, and quick as I had been in getting to the Washington Place door, the flames were already blazing fiercely and spreading fast. If we couldn't get out we would all be roasted alive. The locked door that blocked us was half of wood, the upper half was thick glass. Some girls were screaming, some were beating the door with their fists, some were trying to tear it open. Someone broke out the glass part of the door with something hard and heavy, I suppose the head of a machine. I climbed or was pulled through the broken glass and ran downstairs to the sixth floor, where someone took me down to the street.

There were two elevators for passengers and two for freight. Workers were forbidden to use the passenger elevators. But they streamed toward them now. A group waiting by the elevator door on the eighth floor shouted in dismay as the elevator passed them and went up to the tenth floor. By now, smoke filled the 150-square-foot (about 14-square-meter) workroom, and flames were everywhere. When the elevator came back, a gush of air from the opening door fed the flames even more.

The elevators held only fifteen people, but more than thirty jammed inside. Operators carried several groups to the street. Some who could not get inside grabbed the cables and held on as the elevator lurched downward. Their weight broke the roof, and the elevator stopped working. Then fire reached the elevator shaft itself.

An elevator at the Triangle Shirtwaist Factory. The fire spread quickly to the shaft when workers, trying to escape, piled onto the elevator roof and it collapsed.

Workers from the tenth floor and those who could reach it were able to escape. As heat and smoke filled the room, they climbed up the stairs to the roof. Workers and students from the building next door, part of New York University, held out ladders and helped them to safety. Many wept with relief.

Other women headed for the fire escape, but fewer than twenty were able to escape this way. The weak old metal could not withstand the heat of the fire or the weight of those scrambling down. As it crumbled, several workers fell; others had to jump.

THOUSANDS OF PEOPLE now packed the streets. Some urged the workers to leap into blankets being held below. But the force of falling bodies ripped the blankets to shreds. People hit the ground, broken and lifeless.

Within six minutes after the fire had started, Engine Company #18 had arrived and installed a high-pressure hose next to the building. Company #72 arrived, along with Hook and Ladder Company #20. Thirty-five pieces of equipment were brought to the scene. Among them were two new horseless vehicles. By then, all three top stories of the building were ablaze. The heat was so extreme, it warped the iron shutters on a building located 20 feet (6 meters) away.

The workers faced a hideous choice—the agony of burning to death or jumping a distance of 80 feet (24 meters). Reporter William Shepherd wrote, "I looked up—saw that there were scores of girls at the windows. The flames from the floor below were beating in their faces." As onlookers watched, aghast, a girl closed her eyes and leaped from the windowsill. A survivor later said that as the girls' skirts caught fire, they would say a prayer, tie a rag around their eyes, and jump. Two, three, four, even five girls jumped together, holding hands. Onlookers were moved by the sight of a young couple who embraced, then plunged to their deaths.

While some firefighters carried hose lines into the building and up the hallway stairs, others tried to catch those who jumped. Firefighters gripped the life nets, some brand new. The men braced themselves, but the weight of so many falling bodies ripped the nets and knocked them down. Engine Company #20 had a special 20-foot (6-meter) net with a tube-steel frame. It, too, broke as several people fell onto it. Victims also fell on the fire hoses, pressing them against the pavement so that the water spurted out weakly.

Many onlookers fainted, and men could be seen weeping. Some observers pushed their way through the crowd to see what was going on. Policemen set up ropes around the building. In all, twenty-five patrol wagons were called to the fire.

Frances Perkins, an officer of the New York Consumer's League, was in the neighborhood that day. She recalled, "I shall never forget the frozen horror which came over us as we stood with our hands on our throats watching that horrible sight, knowing that there was no help."

Firefighters pushed an aerial ladder up the side of the building. It stopped 30 feet (9 meters) below where it was needed. A few girls jumped and grabbed for the ladder but missed it and fell to their deaths. Laddermen then climbed up and scaled their way to the ninth and tenth floors, trying to reach trapped workers. Meanwhile, girls jumped past them, their clothing in flames. In all, fifty-eight people lay dead on the sidewalk.

After chopping down the doors on the ninth floor, firefighters aimed their hoses directly at the fire. It took only about a half hour to put it out.

Bodies of workers lie on the sidewalk as onlookers watch the fire consume the factory.

When firefighters and policemen finally went inside the building, they found blackened skeletons of workers bent over their machines. Thirty-six workers lay inside an elevator shaft. A final count showed that 146 people had died from falls, suffocation, or burning. Hundreds of others were seriously burned, and many were in hospitals. Among the ashes on the eighth floor, firefighters found twenty-four wedding and engagement rings. When the medical examiner saw the young victims, he began sobbing.

Reporter William Shepherd watched as policemen tied numbered tags to the bodies. Then, he remembered that these were the shirtwaist makers: "I recalled their great strike of last year in which these same girls had demanded more sanitary conditions and more safety precautions in the shops. These dead bodies were the answer."

A SHRIEK OF DESPAIR 6

By evening, families and friends of Triangle workers had joined nearly 10,000 others at the scene of the fire. They searched for their loved ones among the survivors and the dead. Some waited all night as men carried the dead down the stairs of the building.

Now and then, anguished moans were heard in the crowd. Many families expressed their grief in Yiddish and Italian. So badly burned and scarred were many victims that they were barely recognizable. People found daughters, sisters, brothers, cousins, wives, or mothers by means of a shoe, a ring, a scorched skirt.

Wooden coffins were ordered for the dead. In the meantime, the bodies were laid on the sidewalk and covered with tarpaulins. Policemen began placing victims in wagons to be taken to the morgue. They arrived at the Twenty-sixth Street pier on New York's East River, a place that was known as Misery Lane.

Two thousand people stood waiting. Groups of twenty at a time were allowed onto the pier to identify loved ones, a slow and miserable task. By Sunday morning, the last bodies had reached the pier. Only forty-three bodies were identified that night. For days, people came to find their dead.

People line up at the morgue to identify the bodies of their loved ones following the Triangle Factory fire.

A relief effort was launched. Local 25 of the International Ladies' Garment Workers' Union collected $120,000 to aid families whose wage earners had died. The mayor of New York appointed a committee to coordinate relief efforts and find out the needs of the victims and their families. The Red Cross also played an active role, collecting more than $100,000. Checks and cash contributions streamed into the relief committee office.

Funerals were planned for those whose identities were known, but seven bodies remained unidentified. A mass funeral was arranged for them. The Waistmakers' Union sponsored that funeral as well as a memorial march to honor the dead workers. New York City officials warned people not to demonstrate on the day of the funeral. But people were determined to march.

APRIL 5, 1911, was a rainy, gray day. Members of sixty trade unions met at Washington Square. A newspaper reported that as marchers reached the Asch Building, a long, drawn-out cry could be heard—"the mingling of thousands of voices."

At about 3:20, the marchers formed lines of eight people abreast and marched behind an empty hearse under the Washington Square Arch and up Fifth Avenue. The streets were draped with purple and black cloths as a sign of mourning, and businesses on the East Side were closed in respect for the dead and their families. Some 400,000 other New Yorkers came out to pay their respects.

The last group of marchers passed under the arch at about six o'clock. An estimated 120,000 workers marched solemnly behind hearses covered with flowers. One banner carried by garment workers read, "We demand Fire Protection."

Louis Waldman was among those who watched the funeral procession. He later wrote, "A mass emotion of sorrow and despair was felt everywhere on the East Side that day. But in the weeks that followed, these emotions gave way to angry questioning and a determination that a similar tragedy must never take place in New York again."

A PROTEST MEETING was held by the New York Women's Trade Union League at the Metropolitan Opera House. People both rich and humble crowded the hall. Speakers expressed anguish at the tragic fire and called for reforms in factory inspection laws. Rose Schneiderman took the podium, saying,

> This is not the first time girls have been burned alive in the city. Every week I must learn of the untimely death of one of my sister workers. Every year thousands of us are maimed. The life of men and women is so cheap and property is so sacred. . . . I know from experience that it is up to the working people to save themselves. The only way they can save themselves is by a strong working-class movement.

Aroused people also gathered for a meeting in the Cooper Union auditorium to talk about the fire and the problems of working people. Among the crowd were family members of the people who had died. Those at the meeting later recalled the unusually solemn mood. Nobody smiled, and people did not engage in casual greetings or small talk. Leon Stein, author of *The Triangle Fire,* wrote that the hall was filled with anger and grief, that it echoed with "a single, mass shriek of despair."

People began to speak. Among them was woman's rights leader and suffragist Dr. Anna Shaw, who said,

Every man and woman is responsible. . . . You men— forget not that you were responsible! As voters it was your business and you should have been about your business. If you are incompetent, then in the name of heaven, stand aside and let us try. There was a time when woman worked in the home with her weaving, her sewing, her candlemaking. All that has been changed. Now she can no longer regulate her own conditions, her own hours of labor. She has been driven into the market with no voice in laws and powerless to defend herself. The most cowardly thing that men ever did was when they tied woman's hands and left her to be food for the flames.

Morris Hillquit, a former sweatshop worker who had become a lawyer, rose to speak. Hillquit talked about how many workers had suffered a cruel death because of fires or unsafe machinery. He urged the audience to protest not as an angry mob but in a way that would change the laws. At the end, he said, "The greatest monument we can raise to the memory of our 146 dead is a system of legislation which will make such deaths hereafter impossible."

After the Triangle fire, the New York *Evening Journal* featured a picture of a dead shirtwaist worker lying on the pavement. The caption read: "Is any one to be punished for this?"

Many others were discussing who was to blame for the fire and what should be done. These questions were raised by government officials, city council members, journalists, and the citizens of New York. People spoke out against poor working conditions and unsafe factories. It was not only the flames that killed workers, they said. It was greed, weak laws, and criminal abuse of the fire and safety codes. Factory owners and managers exploited workers who could not risk losing their jobs.

Some owners began improving their factories. They said they had not known what was going on, having left the day-to-day management to others. Aware of the criticism against factory owners, the National Association of Manufacturers held a meeting to discuss safety measures.

The Triangle's owners, Max Blanck and Isaac Harris, were widely criticized. They offered to pay the families of dead workers the amount of one week's pay. Writing in *Life and Labor*, Martha

Bensley Bruere scoffed at this idea. She said that the owners acted "as though it were summer and they are giving [the workers] a vacation!" Twenty-three of the families who had lost members in the fire sued the building owner for breaking the fire laws. Lawyers settled the case by giving each family $75.

Blanck and Harris had quickly moved their shirtwaist business to another building. Days after the fire, they placed a notice in the newspaper to tell customers that the Triangle factory was still operating. When inspectors visited the new factory in late March, they found two rows of sewing machines blocking the workers' access to fire escapes. Besides that, the building was not fireproof.

Meanwhile, people urged the city government to pass stricter fire laws and to enforce laws that already existed. Union leaders pointed out that the city would not even admit that many large buildings were being used to house factories. City records in 1911 did not list any factories located in downtown New York.

Society was also to blame, people said. Too many had ignored the plight of workers for too long. And not just in New York City—every year about 50,000 workers in America were dying in work-related accidents or fires, an average of 136 a day.

Shortly after the fire, Edward Croker resigned as Fire Chief of New York City. He announced that he would devote himself to improving safety conditions and finding ways to prevent fires.

A number of people thought the Triangle's owners should be punished. In April, Max Blanck and Isaac Harris were ordered to stand trial for first- and second-degree manslaughter. They decided to promote their point of view with a $1 million advertising campaign. But newspapers refused to take their money or run the ads. Their trial began in December 1911. As the two men walked into the courthouse, people rushed forward, shouting, "Murderers!" Some held out pictures of their dead children.

In the end, Blanck and Harris were found "not guilty." The jury had been told that the men could only be found guilty if: 1) they believed that all the doors in the factory had been locked at all times during the workday; 2) the owners knew they were locked; and 3) the deaths would not have occurred if the doors had not been locked. As expected, many people were shocked by the verdict.

During that time, reformers became even more determined to improve factory conditions. They realized that workers were killed, hurt, and disabled by various things—accidents, poisoning, poor ventilation and sanitation, and too many hours on the job. The Women's Trade Union League asked workers in various factories to fill out a questionnaire about safety conditions, such as fire escapes, and fire hazards, such as oily rags. The questionnaires were kept secret so that employers did not know who had spoken out.

Within a year of the fire, New York State published a three-thousand-page report called *Corrupt Practices in Insurance Companies*, which listed abuses in the fire insurance industry. New York became the first of many states to pass new fire laws. In October 1911, the Sullivan-Hoey Fire Prevention Law came into effect. This set up a single Fire Commission with more power than before. It required owners of factory buildings to install sprinkler systems. A Division of Fire Prevention was also set up.

Across the nation, people read about the Triangle fire. Other states changed their laws, too. Numerous factory safety codes, building codes, and fire prevention laws with stiffer penalties were passed during the next few years. Upset about the young ages of many workers, people worked harder to change child labor laws.

Max Blanck (left) and Isaac Harris,
owners of the Triangle Shirtwaist Factory,
were indicted on first- and second-degree
manslaughter charges. Following their
trial, they were found "not guilty."

The Citizens Committee on Safety organized a Fire Prevention Bureau in New York. It included some of the best-known men in the city. The committee stated that anyone who opened a factory must notify the state. The state could not inspect a factory and enforce the laws if it did not even know where factories were operating. The Department of Labor added more inspectors, to check factories more often. Fire drills and fire-prevention measures were now required. Women were no longer allowed to work at night in factory buildings.

In June 1911, the New York State Factory Investigating Commission was appointed to study factory safety. Headed by State Senator Robert E. Wagner, it included Samuel Gompers, WTUL President Mary Dreier, Rabbi Stephen Wise, Rose Schneiderman, and Frances Perkins. The commission inspected numerous factories and tenement buildings and met with safety experts. For four years, the commission's work continued. By 1914, thirty-six new laws had been passed at their suggestion. The fifty-four-hour workweek became a New York state law in 1913. And a new industrial code was enacted.

WTUL members, led by such members as Rose Schneiderman, set out to inform workers about the new laws. They held meetings outdoors at lunchtime and in the evening. They urged workers to report any violations of the laws.

The struggle of the workers, especially women workers, went on. In 1914, the WTUL founded the School for Active Workers in the Labor Movement. A few women became full-time employees at the school and were paid to organize labor activities. Through the years, the school trained many labor leaders.

THESE YEARS—from 1900 to 1920—became known as the Progressive Era, because of the many reforms that took place. By 1912, states had begun passing laws to provide for a minimum wage for women. But this wage was often so low that women could afford only the bare necessities of life. Many people still held the

Fifty years after the Triangle Shirtwaist Factory fire, survivors gathered to remember those who had died and to renew the vow to prevent similar tragedies in the future.

TRIANGLE FIRE

ON THIS SITE, 146 WORKERS LOST THEIR LIVES IN
THE TRIANGLE SHIRTWAIST COMPANY FIRE ON
MARCH 25, 1911. OUT OF THEIR MARTYRDOM CAME
NEW CONCEPTS OF SOCIAL RESPONSIBILITY AND
LABOR LEGISLATION THAT HAVE HELPED MAKE AMERICAN
WORKING CONDITIONS THE FINEST IN THE WORLD

INTERNATIONAL LADIES' GARMENT WORKERS' UNION

idea that women were working for extra money, while men had to support families. Years more would pass before wages for women workers really improved.

The International Ladies' Garment Workers' Union continued to grow. By 1916, it was strong enough to support a walkout of 25,000 workers in New York City, then a fourteen-week strike that involved 2,000 shops and 60,000 union workers. After 1917, more women served in leadership roles in the union.

After World War I ended in 1918, Congress set up a Women's Bureau. Its purpose was to "promote the welfare of wage-earning women, improve their working conditions, increase their efficiency, and advance their opportunities for profitable employment."

More changes were to come after Franklin D. Roosevelt became U.S. president in 1933. Roosevelt introduced many programs and laws to give more security to the working poor and to retired workers. He signed the National Labor Relations Act in 1935. It legalized collective bargaining between unions and employers. He also appointed the first woman cabinet member, Frances Perkins, as Secretary of Labor. Perkins had witnessed the Triangle fire and had been part of the investigating committee that followed.

In 1961, Perkins spoke at a fiftieth anniversary meeting in memory of the Triangle victims. She recalled how the fire had stirred the public conscience and led people to work together to pass laws that would prevent such disasters in the future. At the end, Perkins said of those who had lost their lives that day in 1911, "They did not die in vain and we will never forget them."

CHRONOLOGY

1790   Samuel Slater opens his first textile mill in Rhode Island; many of the employees are children.

1799   A Philadelphia shoemakers' union holds the first well-organized strike. Within a few years, miners also strike.

1824   Women weavers in Pawtucket, Rhode Island, join male workers to protest a wage cut and longer working hours.

1825   Women form the United Tailoresses Society of New York.

1831   The United Tailoresses Society of New York holds the first strike for American women workers.

1864   Sewing women in New York City form the Working Women's Union (WWU). Sewing women in several other cities also begin to organize.

1865   Workers and prominent citizens in New York City form the Working Women's Protective Union (WWPU).

1866   The National Labor Union (NLU) is formed.

1869	The Knights of Labor, an early labor union, is started in Philadelphia by Uriah Stephens.
1870	A woman is elected second vice president of the National Labor Union.
1886	The American Federation of Labor is formed.
1900	Women from different garment trades unite to form the International Ladies' Garment Workers' Union (ILGWU).
1901	The Triangle Shirtwaist factory opens for business.
1905	Middle- and upper-class women reformers join workers to start the Women's Trade Union League (WTUL) in New York City.
1906	Local 25 Waistmakers' Union, a branch of the ILGWU, is formed. Triangle workers are warned not to join.
1908	Shirtwaist workers leave their jobs to protest long hours, poor wages, and dangerous working conditions.
1909	In November, thousands of shirtwaist workers begin a large-scale strike that will last nearly three months.
1911	On March 25, fire breaks out in the Triangle factory, resulting in 146 deaths and many injuries. In June, the New York State Factory Investigating Commission is appointed; by 1914, thirty-six new laws would be passed.
1912	States begin passing minimum wage laws for women workers.
1913	The fifty-four-hour workweek becomes law in New York State.
1935	Under President Franklin Roosevelt, the National Labor Relations Act becomes law.

FURTHER READING

Bader, Bonnie. *East Side Story*. New York: Kaleidoscope Press, 1993.

Cavanah, Frances, ed. *We Came to America*. Philadelphia: MacRae Smith, 1954.

Chan, Rhoda. *No Time for School, No Time for Play*. New York: Messner, 1972.

Garrison, Webb. *Disasters That Made History*. Nashville: The Abingdon Press, 1973.

Goldin, Barbara Diamond. *Fire!: The Beginnings of the American Labor Movement*. New York: Viking, 1992.

Higham, John. *Strangers in the Land*. New York: Atheneum, 1963.

Kartman, Ben and Leonard Brown, eds. *Disaster!* New York: Pellegrini and Cudahy, 1948.

Maloney, William E. *The Great Disasters*. New York: Grosset & Dunlap, 1976.

Mann, Arthur. *Immigrants in American Life*. Boston: Houghton Mifflin, 1968.

Meltzer, Milton. *Bread—And Roses: The Struggle of American Labor, 1865–1915*. New York: Knopf, 1967.

Morrison, Joan, and Charlotte Fox Zabusky. *American Mosaic: The Immigrant Experience in the Words of Those Who Lived It*. New York: Dutton, 1980.

Riis, Jacob. *Children of the Tenements*. New York: Scribner's, 1903.

Rips, Gladys Nadler. *Coming to America*. New York: Delacorte, 1981.

Werstein, Irving. *The Great Struggle: Labor in America*. New York: Scribner's, 1965.

BIBLIOGRAPHY

Arnott, Teresa, and Julie Matthaei. *Race, Gender, and Work: A Multicultural Economic History of Women in the United States.* Boston: South End Press, 1991.

Bernheimer, Charles. *The Shirtwaist Strike.* New York: University Settlement Series, 1910.

Blewett, Mary. *Men, Women, and Work.* Urbana: University of Illinois Press, 1988.

Brooks, Thomas R. *Toil and Trouble: A History of American Labor.* New York: Delacorte, 1971.

Clevely, Hugh. *Famous Fires.* New York: John Day, 1958.

Corbett, Edmund V. *Great True Stories of Tragedy and Disaster.* New York: Arco, 1961.

Ditzel, Paul C. *Fire Engines, Firefighters.* New York: Crown, 1976.

Dulles, Foster Rhea. *Labor in America.* New York: Crowell, 1966.

Dye, Nancy Shrom. *As Equals and as Sisters: Feminism, Unionism, and the Women's Trade Union League of New York.* Columbia: University of Missouri Press, 1980.

Eisenstein, Sarah. *Give Us Bread but Give Us Roses: Working Women's Consciousness in the United States, 1890 to the First World War.* London: Routledge & Kegan Paul, 1983.

Ewen, Elizabeth. *Immigrant Women in the Land of Dollars: Life and Culture on the Lower East Side, 1890–1925.* New York: Monthly Review Press, 1985.

Foner, Philip S. *American Labor Songs of the Nineteenth Century*. Urbana: University of Illinois Press, 1975.

―――. *Women and the American Labor Movement: From the First Trade Unions to the Present*. New York: Free Press, 1982.

Glenn, Susan. *Daughters of the Shtetl*. Ithaca, N.Y.: Cornell University Press, 1990.

Haywood, Charles Fry. *General Alarm*. New York: Dodd, 1967.

Henry, Alice. *The Trade Union Woman*. New York: D. Appleton, 1915.

Hymowitz, Carol, and Michaele Weissman. *A History of Women in America*. New York: Bantam Books, 1978.

Kessler-Harris, Alice. *A Woman's Wage: Historical Meanings and Social Consequences*. Lexington: University Press of Kentucky, 1990.

―――. *Out to Work: A History of Wage-Earning Women in the United States*. New York: Oxford University Press, 1982.

Lerner, Gerda. *The Female Experience: An American Documentary*. Indianapolis: Bobbs-Merrill Education, 1977.

Levine, Louis. *The Women's Garment Workers*. New York: Arno Press, [1924] 1969.

Lilienthal, Meta Stern. *From Fireside to Factory*. New York: Macmillan, 1910.

Malkiel, Theresa Serber. *Diary of a Shirtwaist Striker*. Ithaca, N.Y.: ILR Press, 1990.

Milkman, Ruth, ed. *Women, Work, and Protest: A Century of U.S. Women's Labor History*. London: Routledge & Kegan Paul, 1985.

Morris, John V. *Fires and Firefighters*. Boston: Little, Brown, 1953.

O'Sullivan, Judith, and Rosemary Gallick. *Workers and Allies: Female Participation in the American Trade Union Movement, 1824–1976*. Washington, D.C.: Smithsonian Institution, n.d.

Pelling, Henry. *American Labor*. Chicago: University of Chicago Press, 1960.

Powderly, Terence. *The Path I Trod*. New York: Columbia University Press, 1940.

Rayback, Joseph G. *A History of American Labor*. New York: Free Press, 1966.

Riis, Jacob. *How the Other Half Lives*. New York: Scribner's, 1890.

Robinson, Harriet H. *Loom and Spindle: Life Among the Early Mill Girls*. Kailua, Hawaii: Press Pacifica, 1976.

Schneider, Dorothy, and Carl J. Schneider. *Women in the Progressive Era*. New York: Facts on File, 1993.

Schneiderman, Rose, with Lucy Goldthwaite. *All For One*. New York: Paul S. Eriksson, 1967.

Sklar, Kathryn Kish, and Thomas Dublin. *Women and Power in American History*. Englewood Cliffs, N.J.: Prentice Hall, 1991.

Sochen, June. *Herstory: A Woman's View of American History*. New York: Alfred Publishing Co., 1974.

Solden, Norbert C., ed. *The World of Women's Trade Unionism*. Westport, Conn.: Greenwood Press, 1985.

Stein, Leon, ed. *Out of the Sweatshop: The Struggle for Industrial Democracy*. New York: Quadrangle, 1977.

———. *The Triangle Fire*. Philadelphia: Lippincott, 1962.

Sweet, James A. *Women in the Labor Force*. New York: Seminar Press, 1973.

Taft, Philip. *Organized Labor in American History*. New York: Harper and Row, 1960.

Tax, Meredith. *The Rising of the Women; Feminist Solidarity and Class Conflict, 1880–1917*. New York: Monthly Review Press, 1980.

Tripp, Annie Huber. *The I.W.W. and the Paterson Silk Strike of 1913*. Urbana: University of Illinois Press, 1987.

Waldman, Louis. *Labor Lawyer*. New York: Dutton, 1945.

Wertheimer, Barbara Mayer. *We Were There: The Story of Working Women in America*. New York: Pantheon, 1977.

Zophy, Angela Howard, and Frances M. Kavenik, eds. *Handbook of American Women's History*. Hamdon, Conn.: Garland, 1990

INDEX

Page numbers in *italics* refer to illustrations.

African Americans, 14, 24, 25, 34
American Federation of Labor
    (AFL), 24, 28
Anderson, Mary, 28
Anthony, Susan B., 23-24
Apprenticeship, 24
Asch Building, *6*, 7, *9*, 36
Asians, 25

Belmont, Mrs. O.H.P., 28
Blacklisting, 26
Blanck, Max, 34, 49-51, *52*
Bruce, M. Linn, 36
Bruere, Martha Bensley, 49-50

Child labor, 11, *12*, 13, 15, 16, 51
Citizens Committee on Safety, 52
Collective bargaining, 19, 55
Contract system, 22

Corrupt Practices in Insurance Compa-nies, 51
Cosmopolitan Club, 34
Croker, Edward, 35-36, 50

Diary of a Shirtwaist Striker (Mal-kiel), 33-34
Diamond Waist Company, 35
Dreier, Mary, 32-33, 53

Fire insurance industry, 51

Gompers, Samuel, 31, 53

Harris, Isaac, 34, 49-51, *52*
Henry, Alice, 29
Hillquit, Morris, 48

Immigrants, 8, 13, 25
International Ladies' Garment Work-ers' Union (ILGWU), 28, 29, 34, 46, 55

Inventions, 25
"Ironclads," 26

Knights of Labor, 24

Labor Department, 28-29, 52
Labor movement, 10, 19-24, *21*, 26
Labor Standards, The, 22
Ladies' Industry Association, 20
Legal aid, 22
Lemlich, Clara, 17, 31-32
Leo XIII, Pope, 25
Leslie's Illustrated Weekly, 14-15
Lieserson Company, 34
Life and Labor, 49
Lifschitz, Dinah, 37
Lincoln, Abraham, *22*
Living conditions, 10, 13-14, 18, *23*
Lowell, Massachusetts, 13, 20
Lowell Female Labor Reform Association, 20

Malkiel, Theresa, 33-34
Miners, 19
Minimum wage, 53

National Association for the Advancement of Colored People (NAACP), 34
National Association of Manufacturers, 49
National Labor Relations Act (1935), 55
National Labor Tribune, 23

National Labor Union (NLU), 23-24
Native Americans, 14
Newman, Pauline, 15-18, 32, 33
New York Sun, 22
New York Trades' Assembly, 21

Overtime, 17, 33
Ovington, Mary White, 34

Pawtucket, Rhode Island, 20
Perkins, Frances, 41, 53, 55
Picketing, 29, 31, 32
Piecework, 11, 17
Powderly, Terence, 24
Printers, 19
Progressive Era, 53

Red Cross, 46
Reform movement, 10, 51-53
Rest rooms, 29
Roosevelt, Eleanor, 28
Roosevelt, Franklin D., 55

Safran, Rosie, 37-38
Schneiderman, Rose, 29, 47, 53
School for Active Workers in the Labor Movement, 53
Sewing Girls Union of Chicago, 24
Sewing women, 14
Shaw, Anna, 48
Shepherd, William Gunn, 8, 40, 43
Shirt Sewers' Cooperative Union, 24
Shirtwaists, 7, 17, *18*, 33

[63]

Shoemakers, 19
Slater, Samuel, 11
Slums, 13
Stein, Leon, 47
Stephens, Uriah, 24
Strikes, 19-21, *21*, 29, 31-34, 43, 55
Suffragists, 23
Sullivan-Hoey Fire Prevention Law, 51
Sweatshops, defined, 14

Tenements, 10, 13-14, 18
Textile factories, 11, 13
Trade unions, 10, 19-21, 23, 26, 28
Trade Union Woman, The, 29, 31
Transportation, 25
Triangle Fire, The (Stein), 47
Triangle Shirtwaist Company, 15-16, 29, 31-34, 36
　　fire, 7-8, *9*, 10, 36-38, *39*, 40, 41, *42*, 43, 44, *45*, 46-48, *54*, 55

U.S. Industrial Commission, 25

United Tailoresses Society of New York, 20

Voting rights, 23

Wages, 10, 11, 13-15, 17, 18, 22, 24, 34, 53, 55
Wagner, Robert E., 53
Waistmakers' Union, 46
Waldman, Louis, 8, 47
Welcome Workingman, 22-23
Wise, Stephen, 53
Women's Bureau, 28-29, 55
Women's Journal, 21
Women's Trade Union League (WTUL), 28-29, 31, 32, 47, 51, 53
Workday, 14, 20, 25
Workingman's Advocate, The, 22
Working Women's Protective Union (WWPU), 22, 23
Working Women's Union (WWU), 20, 21
Workweek, 32-34